Monstrance

Monstrance

poems by
Sarah Klassen

TURNSTONE PRESS

Monstrance
copyright © Sarah Klassen 2012

Turnstone Press
Artspace Building
206-100 Arthur Street
Winnipeg, MB
R3B 1H3 Canada
www.TurnstonePress.com

Turnstone Press gratefully acknowledges the assistance of the Canada
Council for the Arts, the Manitoba Arts Council, the Government of
Canada through the Canada Book Fund, and the Province of Manitoba
through the Book Publishing Tax Credit and the Book Publisher
Marketing Assistance Program.

Printed and bound in Canada by Friesens for Turnstone Press.

Library and Archives Canada Cataloguing in Publication

Klassen, Sarah, 1932–
        Monstrance / Sarah Klassen.

Poems.

ISBN 978-0-88801-392-7

        I. Title.

PS8571.L386M66 2012   C811'.54   C2012-901578-4

Contents

You yourself are even another little world
and have within you the sun and the moon and even the stars.
Origen

Monstrance

This nascent hour

(January 1, 2009)

Two horses on the morning of the first day!
Bodies like monuments, jet coats coarse and thick.
Between them, power to pull a wagon piled with hay bales,
haul through waist-deep, freshly fallen snow
a load of hyper-active birthday-celebrating children.
These animals could budge a stone boat heaped with rocks
that erupt in spring like mushrooms, move frozen manure,
pull the plough that breaks ground where pioneers
felled poplar, birch, oak, hacked stubborn undergrowth.
They could be hoisted high, lowered into the hold of a ship.
Picture them dragging a field kitchen to the front line,
tumbrels to the guillotine. Imagine them galloping,
war horses hitched to a fiery chariot,
hell-bent for glory.

I stood at the window and stared.
I nearly dropped my coffee.

Corralled between a bunch of banged-up vehicles
and the closed back door of a shabby bungalow,
the pair paced back and forth, back and forth,
travellers impatient for departure, they strode
in opposite directions, turned, retraced their heavy steps
and when they met, stood still, became one merged,
amorphous shape, a silhouette, an optical illusion,
Rorschach ink blot sent to test me, then pulled apart
the way you might pull felted wool apart
and became again a pair.

Where on earth were they from?

I wanted to wake the neighbourhood—adults, kids, dogs—
call the cops, the media. But at this nascent hour
who would answer? Who would believe me?

The snow-draped derelict cars were frosted birthday cakes:
gouged metal, splintered glass, rust patches
covered over. The bungalow's back door, closed.
The inhabitants dormant.

Sun had risen. I should have grabbed a camera,
boots, marched down the narrow lane to look.
Instead I rang my neighbour, rousing her
to be my witness. She said, Oh! Hung up,
went back to bed. I couldn't. I conjured
that quartet of ominous, apocalyptic horses,
the black one representing famine. Folly to ponder
death by pestilence, hunger, sword on such a morning,
sun transforming back yards into fields of diamonds.

I watched the animals move close together, friends
comforting each other, waiting for someone to lead them
out of the scrap metal wasteland, out of winter
into pasture. They knew no more than I
what this new year, this brilliant day, the imminent hour
held of grief or glory.

I forgot my coffee.

How still my two good horses had become.
How adamant their ink black coats against the snow.

I. Travel Advisory

One's destination is never a place, but a new way of seeing things.
Henry Miller

Monstrance

(An exhibition of church treasure, Vilnius, 2001)

Fountains on the morning boulevard declare praise.
Garish geraniums, plump tulips, tipsy songbirds
burst with it. The city stirs. The church unveils
—triumphantly—a stunning inventory:

>Bronze candlesticks, altar cloths
>embroidered with gilt thread,
>vestments, ornate crucifixes, jewel-
>encrusted chalices, gold-plated cups,
>chasubles, ponderous monstrances.

What is a monstrance *for*? A prairie tourist
wandering in wonders.
Webster says:
>*A vessel in which the consecrated host*
>*is exposed to receive the veneration*
>*of the faithful.*

Like the desperate housewife in the parable
who swept her house for one lost coin,
the tourist searches niches for a mustard seed of faith,
the fist-sized cup of a thumping heart for vestiges
of consecration, a bubbling up, a slender
sacrifice of praise.

***

Accumulation of sacred artefacts
—chalices, crowns, vessels—
began when Lithuania was baptized,
1387. Vigilance began too.
One-half the hoarded treasure plundered
on the road to Koenigsberg for safe-keeping,
mid-seventeenth century. The rest entrusted
to the fastness of a duke's castle
and in 1667 borne home victorious
to Vilnius.

Past the recovered dazzle: the sombre
painting of a saint in plain robes
alone in a flowerless meadow, a scene
to soothe the overwhelmed eye. A reprieve
from gold that wants to outshine the sun,
out-glitter the midnight sky, the yellow prairie
wheat ripe for cutting. A harvest
safely stored.

***

World War Two: the sacred treasures
bricked in under the cathedral,
safe from Soviets and thieves.
Preserved by quality and providence

from rust. Rescued
like saints from tribulation,
they rested in the cool, dark crypt.
1985: someone remembered

or during renovation stumbled
by accident upon them. Dug them up.
Imagine the rejoicing when the lost was found,
a fountain spurt of gratitude. An exultation.

Songbirds stitched into tapestry
hover meticulously over saints,
long-faced patrons, all twelve disciples,
Christ in a sombre robe.

Allowed to look, the tourist wants to touch,
be touched,
but everything is out of bounds: saints, angels,
Christ, even the hem of a garment.

***

A guide provides commentary in a language
the tourist cannot comprehend.
How should ponderous matter contain spirit,
the mortal, immortality?

Try holding in your mind the mystery
of word made flesh, dwelling for a while among us.
The divine divested of divinity. The invisible made visible.
Mystery confounds plain language (*this* is real and *that*

illusion). You are afraid you might be dreaming,
afraid a crucifix is just an object subject to corruption,
crowns, candlesticks mere artefacts.
Gold only gold.

***

Downstairs the treasures are rough-hewn,
indifferently guarded. Primitive figures
the country's artisans in a lull from war
sculpted from lime tree trunks.

You move among the wooden forms
as if you are in a forest. As if
you have found friends. Mary and Martha,
eleven apostles, Jesus

with imperfectly carved eyes. Pensive,
he rests his head on a weathered hand,
perches like any careworn peasant on a stump.
Taking a break, taking stock, recalling

words that blazed from his mouth:
about moths;
about corrosive properties of rust;
tips for storing wealth. Also

the abbreviated story of a person
who discovered buried treasure
and with joy sold everything
and bought that field.

***

Before you leave, linger
before this burnished tray. Surface like glass,
and yet your face, reflected, is imperfect.
An artist with a steady hand might smooth
the troubled brow, modify the elongated chin,
bloodless mouth, curiously wavering eyes.

But the silver tray is guarded, plexiglas
on every side. Try to trace
with a moist and surreptitious finger
on glass, on air, small emendations,
longing for what's lost. Treasure
too deeply buried or too fervently desired.

The bell tolls.
Treasure-seekers, satisfied or not, must leave
silver and gold, a country's history, the church's
exhibition.
 (Any child, the city's poor, its thieves,
may come and see.) With empty hands,

you step into the empty street and breathe the evening in.
Shafts of light fall on the fountain, on tulips, beds of rue.
Geraniums on the boulevard bloom bright as blood.

Purim

(Museum in Vilnius, 2001)

Each year some lucky Lithuanian Jewish girl
played Queen Esther, bore the fantastic crown,
the weight of destiny and duty.
She was beautiful, virtuous enough,
loved life.

Easy to cast the king. Ahasuerus
built his citadel in Susa,
loved women, was rich, apparently
willing to take advice,
but still the king.

Haman, who ordered gallows built for Mordechai the Jew,
was himself hanged on them. Justice seen to be done,
Shalom restored, it seemed,

but Haman isn't really dead.
In every century, in every country Jews whisper
news of him, warnings that come too late.
Resurrected, Haman herds them into ghettos,
drives them like cattle into forests

near Vilnius. On quiet evenings you can hear
the dull echo of guns, Queen Esther weeping.
Leaves, their tongues unfolded by a rasping wind,
whisper on cue: *Shalom   Shalom   Shalom.*
Is it a benediction? A final, futile warning?
A farewell?

Guide to the KGB Museum
(Vilnius, 2001)

The courthouse door slams shut behind you
like a gunshot. A sentence against light.
Stone steps descend to the cells' dark territory,
a clammy underworld. A bitter country
that you, free traveller, not guiltless, but not yet condemned,
selected from museums listed in the latest
Vilnius in Your Pocket.

Prisoners with empty pockets slept
empty of hope
on unrelenting beds, walls dripping
moisture like bleached blood.

Ice water fills the concrete basin in the torture cell.
Spent from interrogation, taunts, repeated beatings,
lack of sleep, the depleted body,
well-worn punching bag,
with one dull splash
falls in.

A guardroom is a prison too: guards forced
to restrain, deprive, grind down
the breathing dead, who hold
eternity in pulsing hearts.

A narrow corridor, a row of peepholes
straight from a Solzhenitsyn novel. Trapdoors
to squeeze tin bowls of watery gruel through.
Soup with fish heads.
Dry bread. The heartsick, hollow prisoner will take
and eat.

For the inmate gone berserk with memory:
gestures, touch of living loved ones, glances,
doubts of innocence,
the walls in this next cell are padded.
Solitude without solace.

The doomed lie sleepless
on the eve of execution. Bleak rooms
crammed with emptiness. No space
for tables, chairs, false hope
of deliverance. No room
for light.

En route to death, the condemned
cross (shackled) a fenced-in yard:
scant metres of earth, the rationed sky, a quick
snatch of air that holds the agonized
sweet scent of home.

Now slip these grey shrouds over your shoes.
You will walk on sacred ground. On grief. On glass
through which a bed of sand is visible. Bones
buried like history in dust. Scraps of cloth,
leather that might have been a belt.

Pockmarks in the concrete wall:
bullets that flesh and bone could not resist
set like jewels in cement.
All hope (abandoned in a structure built
for justice) stopped here.

Blood has been washed away
but the stench endures. It mingles with the sweet
perfume of lilacs, lilies of the valley, yellow roses
hawked in the cobbled city streets.
It clings to your skin. You can smell it
in the chestnut trees that every spring
lift candles to the sky.

Water Songs

1. Prayer in time of too much rain on the prairie
(June, 2010)

Let some of it fall on the Negev where travellers
press noses to bus windows: a slender landscape
leached of colour.

Let some of it fall on dusty roadside camels,
on silhouetted sheep, shepherds in sand-
storms that obliterate the world.

Let it descend, a deluge, on the shrinking Dead Sea,
the River Jordan dwindling down to a narrow prairie creek.
Top up the turbulent Sea of Galilee.

Let rain fill barrels on flat-roofed houses in the West Bank,
let them overflow the way those ancient *mikvehs*
overflowed with rainwater.

Remember the years of prairie drought when the slender
panting deer burst forth from dry bush
into dry clearing: wild-eyed
and thirsty.

2. Thirsty

(A woman, a Samaritan, came to draw water. John 4:7)

A woman rests at midday on the edge
of the well, catches her breath,
lowers the rope, her empty bucket fills.
The temperature will not stop climbing.
Her face, once pretty, sags.

What will she cook for supper? Will the fire
still flicker when she returns? Will neighbours
cast sideways glances? She might be thinking
of cool, dark evenings, sex, wet weight of water.
Her heavy lids fall shut, her body slumps.

A traveller arrives, a stranger
with no bucket. Nothing much
upsets this woman. This man
wants water and she's flabbergasted,
looks him up and down, lets him drink.

Thirst-quenched, what's there to talk about?
Not politics or the economy. For sure not this
infernal heat. She throws a question out—red herring—
local mountain top or in Jerusalem, where
does a village woman dare to meet the Deity?

What does she know about abstraction:
worship, spirit, holiness? Propriety
has constantly eluded her. Or she eluded it.
Tries to compose her scattered brain,
rein in her wayward heart, her curiosity

about this stranger who appears
to see right through her, speaks to her:
unclean Samaritan, a woman
burdened with an empty bucket,
empty heart. How could anyone know

all she ever wanted, needed,
was to fill her bucket,
drink and drink
and quench her thirst?

3. Petra

Who carves a city out of rock buffeted for eons
by wind-flung dust, sun, devastating downpour?
Rock that won't be shaken. The Nabateans found
a small perennial stream, thin trickle in dry season,
torrent during flash floods. They harnessed it,
built cisterns, dams, conduits, stored water for
their animals. Their children. Trees grew
in this contrived oasis. These people hewed
a city out of rose-red rock.

Tourists with cameras, water bottles, travelling
from the Negev, West Bank, Jezreel Valley,
Hebron—where talk of water is terse—
clamber through excavated tombs, temples,
theatres and royal palaces. Marvellous
how these ambitious ancients controlled
(the way they controlled water) trade routes
in the Middle East, developed a desert economy.
Ruled their world.

        Were they hospitable to alien travellers?
        Would they have dreamt of selling water?
        Or withholding it?

These long-gone, clever people had it all:
entrepreneurship, engineering skills, imagination.
And more: to them was given that small stream,
the source without which only fools
would dare to dream a city.

4. Falcon

There was a woman married a Bedouin.
Blonde, azure-eyed, she left everything
to live in a desert cave. They said
she'd overstepped every allowable limit:
good judgment, niceties of civilization.
Had fallen in love with an Arab's bearing,
the way he rode his horse, his dark, dark eyes,
thrust of his amazing sword.

It wasn't the man and his horse she found
irresistible. Silence and solitude called to her
mornings when the falcon rose from its nest
soaring toward God. The bristling sky at night
revealed all she could bear of unveiled glory.
She grew humble. She discovered:
if you pray without ceasing
—and who wouldn't when the wind-
whipped sand stings you blind,
hides the sun, sifts through everything?—
your knees grow calloused as a camel's
and you desire not so much water
as mercy.

She planted a pistachio tree,
let the desert sun darken her skin,
collected pink, striated stones,
studied choreographies of light and shadow
on sand, on boulders, told stories,
washed her husband's clothes in scant water,
bore his children. One day she stopped
snapping pictures, knowing
they would fade or fail
to reflect one iota of a desert's essence,
a fraction of her astonishment.

Stepping through a rift in the rock
she found herself in Petra,
and understood: nothing
can prepare you for the slender chasm
between splendour and austerity. Here

you learn to live sparingly,
claim only your fair share
of water,
welcome the stranger,
rise early like the solitary falcon,
take all you want of silence,
all you need of love.

5. What you will need at the Galilee

Forget the concrete barriers.
Forget the checkpoints.
Come to the lakeshore.
Sunlight reflected off the water dazzles
and then blinds.
You will need shades.
You will need sunscreen.

***

If you want to escape, embark
in that small fishing boat, cross over
to Capernaum. Bring with you
lots of bottled water.

***

Alternatively, row your boat
to the middle of the lake.
Throw out your net. You will need
a net.

***

On a stormless day join tourists for a pleasure cruise.
The crew will tell you of the scarcity of fish,
government restrictions. When the net's hauled up,
empty, you will need to listen.

***

From that same pleasure craft you'll see
Tiberias, Mount of Beatitude, birds
flitting through orange orchards.
Bring binoculars.
Bring your imagination.

***

Step into the water where it's shallow.
Wade in cautiously. Pick up small stones,
one in each hand. Begin singing.
You will need a song.

***

The rippled water you step out of
is not the water you stepped barefoot into.
(Read Heraclitus.)

***

Come like a pilgrim to the place
where Jordan River leaves the Galilean Sea.
If you desire to be baptized, let it happen
here. You will need a clean white shroud.

***

Go out at evening in a row boat. Go to sleep.
Storm will leave you shaken. And awake.
You will need someone to row that boat.

***

For ultimate adventure, try
walking on water. (It was done here first.)
You will need to step out
of your high-powered speed boat.
You will need to let go.

***

Imagine a fish fry on the lakeshore.
Sun just rising. Make it spontaneous. Or even better:
let someone else bring everything:
fresh-caught fish, bread, wood for the fire.
Water.
Bring nothing but your hunger.
Bring your thirst.

6. Travel advisory

Water is everything but not
every*where*. Before you
enter this wilderness
fill your flask,
carry it close to your heart,
guard it with your body.
Be afraid of the alien
robbed of water. He is hiding
as we speak in the cleft of a rock.
Impossible to hear his footsteps in the sand.
He'll creep up like a desert spectre
from behind, grab you by surprise.
His eyes are flint, his muscles stone,
his thirst beyond imagining.
Because his water flask was stolen,
smashed, his empty hand now grips a gun.

Look out! It's loaded.

Do not imagine that he won't shoot straight.

And never ask him what he carries
in his heart.

7. Checkpoints

In this country
they'll pull you over on the road
at checkpoints. Don't be surprised.
At any ancient city gate they'd stop you,
demand your weapons, water bottle,
everything you carry. Even your name.
You'd have to declare whom you love,
whom hate and whom you long to worship
at the altar of this reconstructed temple
in this heat.

My water flask is empty; yours nearly full
but though I ask, you do not offer.

Or was it you who asked and I, afraid,
refused?

That country we both long for lies ahead.
Anyone may enter. They say
water in the river running through it
is abundant, pure. And also free.
No need for flasks or buckets.
There will be no checkpoints,
no more weeping.

Let's drop our guns, cast off our fear
and go together.

              Take my hand
and in the other, hold this stone.
No! Not to throw. This stone
fits perfectly into your palm.
Look: it is white.
It has your name engraved.

II. Home Invasion

Home is where one starts from. T.S. Eliot

Blankets for Afghanistan

Think of it as worship, poking fine steel
needles in and out of fabric, yanking acrylic
yarn through, invoking reverent knots.
The north wind howls a *miserere*.

Think of it as prayer. Discarded skirts, pants,
draperies cut into squares. A polyester litany,
machine-stitched, matched with plain backing,
pinned to a wooden frame.

Alto, soprano and transcendent descant soar
in gratitude while fingers stitch and knot.
Snow rises like a mountain range.
When they have made their patchwork praise,

swept up the scraps, confessed half-hearted knots,
textiles too scant for cutting, fingers too stiff to hold
a threaded needle, while the weather worsens,
the women pause for supplication:

> Let our blankets arrive before the storm.
> Let them be sufficient for the darkest desert night.
> In every cave, at every godforsaken elevation
> may our patchwork cover the wounded
> and our small knots hold.

The colour purple

Our neighbours have painted their front door
deeply purple. Think pansies, think petunias
and the less alliterative though equally lovely asters,
clematis chasing sunlight up the stuccoed wall.
Purple's an imperial colour. Kings, queens

paired it with gold, spectacular effect, though
never without risk. Think of Charles the First,
think Anne Boleyn in her lonely tower,
Jesus arrayed in a royal robe, flogged
until blood flowed. You see it all the time

in colour on TV: Rwanda and the Balkans, eastern Congo
and the boxing ring. The sharp coercion of guns,
the known world's indifference. But I digress.
The neighbour's door, painted, has become
regal. Women whose hair turns white

wear purple dresses, scarlet hats when stepping out
in style. Would Jesus have preferred purple over the drab
garment soldiers gambled for? Did he mind the pale shroud
friends wrapped him in for burial? In Sunday school
we chanted: 'red and yellow, black and white.'

On CNN a heart-wrenched mother begs for something warm
to wrap around a little body with ballooning belly,
fly-infested eyes. Nothing fancy. Any colour.
Just something soft to cover up the blatant
nakedness. The shameful scandal of this dying.

Birthday party

(December, 2006: execution of SH)

On the evening of the execution our excited children
sprawled in a circle on the carpet, tearing gifts
from wrapping paper, test-driving an armoured vehicle.
They grabbed rainbow crayons, faces appeared
smiling on the page. Their happiness

lit up the room: blue leather rocking chair,
lost socks, debris on the carpet, everything shimmered.
We marvelled how joy grew, outgrew the room,
flew like a sparrow through the open patio door.
Outside: the brittle circle of the moon, the winter night

black as the executioner's hood,
black as the eyes that stared at us and kept on
staring through the rope's rough circle, stupefied,
devoid of hope. We scuttled every newspaper,
turned the TV off. Our noisy

children, while we sang
Happy Birthday,
bravely,
blew every candle out.

When we are old will their glad faces
linger with us?
Or what the rope encircled?
Will we remember how we sent a child
with cake-crumbed lips
to shut the patio door through which
our singing fled?

At home

The house opposite is dark, windows blank
as forgotten dreams, front door and driveway
unilluminated. No one has bothered
to plug in strings of Christmas bulbs
that last night spangled the shrubs and overhang.

You could rattle off a string of reasons
for the darkness. The inhabitants have chosen
sleep instead of supper. The entire household
fallen ill. Someone with intention
cut the cord that carries power to appliances.

Nobody's home.

The dwelling across the narrow street
(you speculate) cannot be empty.
It has become the house of fear and you
will signal from your lit location:
Power is on, cupboards stocked with candles.

In spite of ice-packed snow barring the doors
you have scraped together courage,
vowed to be no more distraught than usual,
resolute, awake, and always
(hopefully) at home.

Home invasion

A child stormed my unguarded kitchen,
commandeered the floor, flung plastic lids
like declarations. A quilted potholder
occupied her hungry mouth, her sticky
hands examined a spatula I dropped,
my tattered canvas shoes.
Brown eyes interrogated everything.
When her baby body collapsed
                    and she slept
her breathing held me captive. My child
(I thought), this kitchen you've invaded
harbours red-hot elements, instruments
that slice, shred, pulverize. It isn't safe
for you. A new millennium has broken out
its weapon capability, death-range of missiles.
There is blood to be shed, warm as the blood
that makes your baby cheeks burn brightly,
pulses when you scream and when your feet
kick against my kitchen floor.

sparrow

first light bounces off the breakfast plates
morning a-sparkle with dew-diamonds
lilac bush alive with chittering sparrows

              this dear dear planet our only
earthly home so beautiful so utterly unsafe we must
with all our might defend post 9/11 against mail bombs
potentially deadly in-flight incidents sabotage
of vital government institutions installations plans plots
stockpiles gun-smuggling drug lords wars we must devise
fail-proof strategies commit ourselves in trust to those
with mighty power to save us those we may place
utter faith in presidents the secret service interpol
we will be vigilant build concrete walls fences
checkpoints no expenses spared no sacrifice too costly
our safety top priority a sacred duty we will give
ear to urgent emails phone calls from vendors
of the latest/best in home protection systems
we won't give up won't be distracted

a bedraggled sparrow
twitters in the lilac bush   o
tiny sparrow
cold winds are blowing
blowing
who
will shelter us

In motion

It's the hour when walkers and wheelchairs crowd the aisles
of city buses. I've got neither, not even a cane. Able,

unencumbered, I'm conveyed from the city's outskirts
over the bridge to its inner life. A queue at the soup kitchen.

The door beneath a Pay Day Loan sign opens, closes.
A midday drunk. Unkempt panhandler. Crouched on pavement

a child plays with a stick and a smooth white stone,
for all the world as if she owns the world. Untroubled,

she ignores the bus and us inside it. Walker and wheelchair
begin their stroll to the exit while the noon sun halos

the raven hair of the girl we've left behind, her animated
shadow cast on asphalt. Like that dark shadow

etched in concrete steps at Hiroshima. It cannot move,
yet moves me, as I move toward my journey's end, afraid

I'll fall as I step from the bus into the city's hottest hour.
A brazen sparrow twitters from the bus shelter.

Wind hurls paper cups and dust. My shadow, like an ashen child,
follows me along the street. The breathless world keeps turning.

Cyclist

A cyclist hurtles toward me on the sidewalk. *Run,*
he snarls and I jump, convinced it's me he means. Or is it
a dog following? No. It's a fine-boned boy, ten or eleven.
Slender. Spent from racing the speeding bicycle. *Run,*
the man (can't be his father, surely, but most likely is)
belts out. *Run all the fucking way.* I step aside
to let the desperate runner, the unreasonable rider pass.

Is this some body-building regimen? Crash course
for competitions? A last-ditch shoring up of Dad's
depleted pride? The making of a proxy masculinity?
The dad's a demon if he planned this crass
lesson for the boy's own good.

It's not the last I'll see of them.
The boy's white, baffled face, the man's flint eyes,
will flare beneath my eyelids in the silence before sleep.
(I should have intervened. I should have called the cops.)
I'll wonder if a mother waited, worried in a kitchen,
cream venetians letting in or keeping out the light.
Friendly or vicious dog.

Sleepless, I'll curse all unfit fathers on fast bikes.
The shepherd who will trade a staff in for a club.
I'll rue all cruelty, all undeserved authority
and, still awake, haul out for scrutiny, from memory:

grey filing cabinets, maps, chalkboards, the sun's
oblique rays falling on child-sized desks, rows of
little bodies, a sea of eyes, a universe
of fear or wonder. Up in front the teacher
doles out lessons that consume the minutes
of the hours of the passing day.

On guard

Two girls straddle the sawed-off branch of an elm,
a giddy elevation, a vantage point
from where the swollen river's visible:

willows thigh-deep in water, current purposeful
and swift. Red squirrels chase each other
up and down a crooked oak

as if there's no tomorrow. The girls hold tight,
giggling their silly glee, their fear of height.
Below them: an extended family from the Philippines

three deep around a picnic table piled with lunch.
A bunch of men at the barbeque, arguing.
Children break free, head off in all directions,

fleeing mothers, anxious aunts who warn them:
Don't go far!
A kid on a bike zips through the northbound drive

at the crosswalk, properly. A pick-up truck stops short,
the driver through the open window snarling:
What the fuck this stupid crosswalk shit!

Did I mention the dad at the base of the elm,
arms akimbo, head tilted back,
eyes on his two girls out on a limb? Did I say

it's early spring, too soon for tulips?
The immigrant women craving columbine,
anemone, delicate coral bells.

The men around the barbeque brew remedies
for a world gone wrong.
(It's not the truck driver's words that shock

but the utter absence of expression on his face.
The eyes' intention veiled by shades.
The granite calm of sunburnt, grizzled cheeks.
The square, steel jaw.)

Angry

Someone left the back door ajar
and a fly intrudes. Bluebottle. An erratic
aircraft carving frantic patterns in space,
cruising a window, tracing the illusion
of freedom. A thud-thud-thud
as it bumps up against the glass.
Does a fly know fear? Deep throb of anger?
Or is panic all it knows of emotion?

I've been angry all day about that
young man born with impediments
he doesn't want. He wants a car, a job,
life outside an institution.
His restless fingers kept tap-
tapping on my table.

How could I say *Don't worry,*
everything will be all right?
Delusive words that paint a blue world rosy,
spawn futile hope
and for a moment, falsely,
fend off rage.

Cruising

My neighbour retires early—
three or four AM, after *Doomsday* and
How to Marry a Millionaire. She might
at midnight back her Honda out
of the garage, drive to the 7-Eleven
for cat food or to Sal's for a snack.
Coming home she confronts a convoy
of cop cars cramming our short street,
blocking driveways. While waiting for
an officer to move a cruiser, she observes
the force in action. Under a street light
two teenaged girls spread-eagled
against gleaming metal, searched, interrogated,
shoved like cargo into the back seat,
hauled away. In late September,
mother raccoon and three masked offspring
cruise the starlit lane for garbage.
Feral eyes reflect the hostile glare
of headlights. One moonless night
the whole nine yards arrives, a furious
nocturnal wailing, lurid lights
pierce the resounding silence.
Someone's life is compromised
or even ending. Suddenly
it's morning and the rest of us
have slept, wrapped in down duvets,
cruising in and out of dreams,
untroubled. Undisturbed.

Bowser moves into the neighbourhood

There he is, tethered to a post in the yard
at the end of the lane, black paper cut-out
flat as flat against the stifling summer afternoon.
A panting, painted shadow. A silhouette.
A concept not quite realized

until he moves within the tether's fixed
limits. Each day he tests the limits,
heart, body taut with yearning,
straining, howling hoarsely, piteously.
Could break your heart.

After supper, when his person runs him
down one lane and up another, where
on earth does Bowser think he's going?
Life's a journey homeward bound, said Hermann
Melville, but does Bowser know that?

Does he dream he'll come at last
to an open road, pristine white
beaches of an ocean's endless shore,
or to that fabled mountain built exclusively
of gristled bone? With any luck

restraints dissolve like fog in sunlight,
sky breaks open, ocean-wide, lake-blue.
A seagull clamped to a rotten log
extends its wings, lifts off, appropriately
terrified when Bowser growls.

Molly Magoo

knows the hand that feeds her,
spreads newspapers to catch droppings,
pets her pretty feathers, clips her claws,
is able also to unlatch the wire gate
and let her go.

Molly lays egg after egg after egg.
A cockatiel, she's nervous when she moults.
Is the hand stroking her neck a warning
or a consolation? One of these days
will one of the eggs hatch? Molly

stares into her pink-edged mirror
as if it's a crystal ball or possibly
she's vain. Turns her head this way and that.
Preens. The glass declares her queen.
When finally those feathers grow back in

she'll fly, a shimmering arrow
shot from the apartment balcony. She'll ride
the air across a vast and turquoise ocean
then light on land swaying with coconut palms
and with her cockatiel eyes, behold

a boundless fantasy of bougainvillea.
A world of pink hibiscus.

Regretfully

You are going on vacation.
In preparation for departure
make a list of everything

you must leave behind:
poppies floating like a colony of orange
moons in motion,

intrepid robins foraging in dew-wet lawns,
that blackbird chorus, mornings
in the neighbour's fragrant linden tree.

Also the jet-black brazen crows—
bad riddance to that rabble,
and the rabbits nibbling at the peas.

On the deck, red geraniums
and blue lobelia will not stop re-inventing
Eden. You must leave it

to the vagaries of wind and sun,
mercy of your neighbour.
You must not hesitate, must not look back.

You have packed
and you are going
on vacation.

III. Songs of Ascent

I walk, I lift up, I lift up heart, eyes,
Down all that glory in the heavens to glean our Saviour;

Gerard Manley Hopkins

Prairieology

Prairie's the preferred home of the gopher.
It slips into an earthen orifice
pops up again, alert
curious
and startled by the merest whiff of danger
once more disappears.

Prairie winds
unhindered
abscond with topsoil
hasten tumbleweed along.

Framed by the oceanic sky
meadowlarks warble: matins, vespers, laud.
Red-winged blackbirds perch, wind-tousled
sentinels on weathered fence posts.

Clouds drift, round-bellied
fantasies across the firmament.
Horizon's elusive thread goes on and on
receding.

Time stands still.

> *O God of prairie grasses*
> *tumbleweed*
> *bleached bison bones*
> *monarch of butterflies*
> *birds gophers the unbridled*
> *wind*

here I stand
roofless
miniscule in this flat vastness
terrified of storm
crack of thunder
lightning's fire-fork.
I am listening
for the wind to lose its bluster
stop howling from the west
breathe gently
whisper through me. Until then
O sovereign of hiding places
shelter me

Songs of Ascent

1. Bear Lake

A modest indentation in the earth, a hollow
gouged out over eons by a giant paw
and filled to the brim with mountain run-off.
A pool you can't help staring into
as if you'll fish out mystery.
No altitude to speak of. Easy
to be light of heart. And glad.
On this wide path anyone can circum-
ambulate the water whistling,
pushing a wheelchair,
lugging fishing gear.
But watch your step. Children
however brave should remain close
to parents. Dogs (the large signs warn)
should not walk unattended.
Let no one dare lower their guard
or travel heedlessly
around Bear Lake.

2. Nymph Lake

You have climbed the gravelled path
up to another level.
Here's your chance to belt out praise
before the next ascent
so steep your lungs will burst.
Sing, sing before you dare another step
or change your mind. Before
this miniature lake's quaint shape
its quietude, its beauty
leave you gasping.
You're out of shape: much more
beached whale than water sprite.
You pant. You vow
in the presence of such magnanimity
—so rare, so undeserved—
to exercise from now on (daily)
offerings of gratitude.

3. Dream Lake

Not any kind of dream. This one:
a metaphor you will not need
to wake from. Options
are fairly simple: climb higher
on the slendered path
or consider beginning
the descent.
The choice is yours
a privilege
that woman in blue shorts
and floppy yellow hat
has temporarily postponed.
She's laid her burdens down
as if she means to stay.
Look at her gazing long
and longingly into the lake
whose water could evaporate
before she's made her mind up.
Has she reached her limit?
Lost all desire? Doesn't dare
to venture higher?
She watches an innocent fish
dangle, impaled, from the line
cast by a sun-burnt tourist
who lugged the necessary
paraphernalia
in his backpack
with effort to this height.

To each his own, she thinks
and sinks content
into a deep and private
reverie.
>Pink lilies shimmer on the surface
of her dream. A miniscule
submerged white stone
catches the light.
And her eye.

4. Emerald Lake

Teenagers from the Bible Camp near Estes Park,
nimble as antelopes, overtake you on the narrow path.
By the time you arrive, tired of climbing, hungry,
they're skipping stones in Emerald Lake.
Jump in, jump in, they dare each other, stripping down
to bathing suits. Their leader wades in first. Waist deep
in frigid water he calls out: *Be brave,*
it's not so awful once you're in.
Scarcely shivering he promises whoever musters courage
to come, step with him into the water, won't regret it.
The shadow of a marmot slips between the stoic
weeds rooted in scant soil.
The teens drape rocks with towels, unpack their lunches
and adore the sun. A few are drawn—by zeal,
by sheer exuberance, or pride, or something more
like terror—to the water's edge.
They hesitate, inch forward, petrified.
Their leader, dripping, hair slicked back, enthusiastic,
holds out a hand to welcome them, as if he means
to baptize adolescent campers, wash them clean.

Glad it isn't your name he is calling, you lift your eyes:
gulls circle the cold, enchanting lake, a flock of
screeching witnesses, curious to see who'll be the first
to volunteer complete immersion
in icy Emerald Lake.

Waterfowl

1.

Gulls,
smug in their numerical superiority,
occupy the sandbar, sunny place of ease,
convenient launching pad. A semi-public
stage where they are always obviously
stars. They grow complacent, knowing
majority opinion overrules opposing
bird voices. Gull demonstrations, fly-bys,
sit-down strikes have clout. They know
gulls vote for gulls.
When have there ever not been gulls
wheeling above the lake, screaming
their adamant opinions,
plummeting, plucking out
the eyes of rotting fish?

2.

Pelicans too
possess an obvious advantage.
They're qualified by virtue of their size,
their white, black, orange uniforms,
to hire out for night club bouncers,
shopping mall security,
sumo wrestlers.
                    But they're kind of shy.
That's why they float in shallow water
near the sandbar but not on it.

The least distraction and they'll execute
their clumsy bird-bolt: bulky bodies
staggering up, flapping for altitude.
They'll straighten their formation,
point pouched bills to the receding
horizon.
                    There they go:
a string of black dots lost in orange
brilliance of the sun ascending.

3.

Joggers
on the morning beach stop
short at the sight of the long
stick-neck of a great blue heron
rising above the whole gull crowd,
above pudgy pelicans and lesser water fowl.
Ungainly wings beat stoically against the sky
at lift-off. The heron with endearing nonchalance
knows how to rise to an occasion. He rises now,
neck crook'd in splendid awkwardness.
He's off to lofty solitude, a private lookout tree.
Rising so high, so far above all circumstances,
he's the consummate observer, disengaged,
cool, beholding with a bright eye:
everything.

Crow quartet

1.

Crow mother, denied the gift of song,
can neither croon nor warble her dusky children
to sleep. But never think that she

resents comparison with nightingales
or finds the rawness of her voice
disturbing. She doesn't care one whit

that poets in their quest for metaphor
belabour her black helmet, black tail
feathers, unpleasantly curved claws.

No one praises her voice. But it's *her*
instrument, she'll employ it any way
she can. Rouse the somnolent neighbourhood,

infuriate the squirrel vying for the crude
nest she cobbled from twigs, leaves, filched
fragments of string.

How dare a wingless creature
eye *her* property, *her* sanctuary, podium
from where with all her jet-black heart she loves

to berate, raucously, the known world?
Crow mother plummets from the heady height
and lands victorious on carrion.

2.

Crow mother's got her two fledglings
out on a limb, scolding, urging them on
with harsh harangue until they inch forward
terrified. Imagine your own mother making you
walk the gangplank. There's no way
but forward. The first one, flapping brand new wings,
gains lift-off, drop-off, clumsy landing on the pavement.
The second clings with baby talons to the branch, then,
hassled by its dark parent, takes heart, takes off
and lands pinion-borne, lucky, on grass.
The proud old bird looks down. Having done her duty,
having shown crow love, she ascends to a greater height
and like a conqueror rasps out a brassy peroration
in praise of motherhood. In praise of her
most excellent accomplishment.

3.

Crow mother buzzes you in the lane. You swear
you felt the air shift, a wing tip actually raked
the crown of your head, and here she comes
again and now you see the reason: In the weeds
an ink-black dying bird. One of her own.
A member of the flock. Sister, brother, offspring,
feathers slack as a windless sail, the limp body
pathetic. Don't expect her to let you pass,
to let this lonely dying go unnoticed.
Outraged, defiant, she will undertake
one last heartbroken fly-by.

4.

Crow mother's on a wire,
a mordant silhouette suspended
between earth and sky,
between rising and swooping
to pluck prey from nest
or dumpster. She knows
gravity, knows
air's uplift
and resistance.
Air is her element: it raises her
above the wide horizon. There
the glorious sun sits, poised
to execute her next escape.

    O crow mother,
    queen of the evening,
    rise.

Discovery

Year after year I've wandered through this meadow,
heard ravens bray their prophecy, felt winter's gusts
and never once by accident or providence, before today
discovered in this seeming-empty field these gentians.

Fringed, bottle, pleated, their blue heads mingle
without fanfare with the wind and weathered grass.
Seven closed blooms on one thick stalk.
Serene. Wild. Unassuming.

The slender trail

1. Senses

This landscape yanks you back to your senses.
Sharp crack of a branch, squeak of skis, poles
clicking on ice, woodpecker's bold hammering.
Woodsmoke signals from the warming hut,
a puff, a shimmer, a scent. Motion is a flitting
chickadee, the raven hovering, the shy deer's
feather-light leap across the narrow trail.
And you, as if you have wings, fly too.
Brain bows to the senses, relinquishes
abstraction, theory, all calculation.
Whatever creased the brow, removed
and what seemed vital, overruled.
   The sky is left. A feather the crow let go.
   Bare arms of aspen and the falling snow.

2. Performance

This morning everything demands a poem:
Sheer purity of snow. Sky crisp as the sea
and as blue. Evergreens: black sentinels;
poplars: skeletons; red-headed woodpeckers:
carpenters at work. Ravens carve spirals
in the unblemished sky. A restless flock
of metaphors comes rushing to the brain
like hordes of data to an empty memory stick.

Let it all go. The poem is this moment, this
park the stage, and you a minor player.
Your role: silence. Let the rhythm find you.
Birds trill a descant. Oak, poplar, ash
clap their empty branches while the mute
sun watches and blue shadows follow you.

3. Illusion 1

The park is monochrome—dull sky,
feathery snow on the stripped branches, black
oak skeletons. But where the ski trail veers
into a clearing, stems of grass poke through
paper whiteness and glow gold. The skiers'
toques, rainbow-coloured jackets brighten
the bleak landscape. Light seeps through overcast,
outlines each groove with a blue shadow.

Gliding, you fall victim to illusion: newly groomed
indentations rise: background becomes foreground.
Try skiing when the grooves are ridges; ridges, valleys.
Can't trust your eyes. But look, look up, ahead,
until your vision is corrected. Brain's equilibrium
restored. The baffling trail made plain.

4. Illusion 2

Something black beside the trail and you think: glove,
the fingers pointing up as if there's a hand still in it.
Final stretch of Lent, snow shrinking, last chance
for a quick glide. Nearer, the object resembles a branch
detached by wind or weight of snow from black spruce.
Still closer it's the awkwardly outspread feathers
of a dead crow's half-wing anchored in snow.
Proximity of black and white startles you, claims
purchase in the cautious consciousness. (A child,
you feared boulders, gnarled roots of oak.) An object
might be an omen thrust in your face as you follow
the slender trail, thinking supper, thinking home.
Thinking: the eye, perverse, can alter landscapes,
change an object's meaning. Slyly shift its shape.

Pileated woodpecker

Sunday morning. Our children shout Hosannas,
wave exuberant palm fronds at the altar,
down the aisle. They follow Jesus—
astride a donkey—through Jerusalem, joyous
procession that within the week draws blood.
The rest of us like stone choose silence.

At the trail head parking lot an afternoon
of chittering sparrows, mud-caked suvs.
We are waxing skis while halfway up a broken oak
a bird, its broad back facing the people
hacks with no-nonsense purpose at the rough-
ridged bark where its vigorous claws find purchase.

The massive, crimson-crested bird
has come so close, almost among us.
Mesmerized we ogle its body,
admire its plumage, the whole
fierce enterprise. Most of us don't recognize
the amazing creature clamped to its wounded tree.

All afternoon we lean into our chosen trail,
follow its winding way into the woods,
gain speed, gain distance from the dying
echo of that patient hammering.

After the fall

That day on Lookout Hill the bald, slick slope down-slanting
from my skis, I bent my knees pushed with the poles, took off
(the wind like steel), gained speed and flew. There where the trail
veers sharply to avoid an oak and coasts through an aspen grove,
I lost control. Waxed skis, poles, limbs a matchstick tangle, ankle
bent beneath excruciating weight of my predicament. Balancing
the short, straight trail to the parking lot against the winding,
longer one I had mapped before the fall, I disentangled stoically,
pain flaming in the strained ankle. Clutching my pre-fall plan
I pressed ahead and made it, limping to the finish. The verdict
at Emergency: not fractured. (But damaged ligaments swell up
and hurt like hell.)

Today, remembering the fall, I choose uncomplicated trails.
Snow lodged like tufts of cotton candy on bare branches of
birch. On stump and rock. The sewing-machine-stitch spoor
of a pocket mouse appears and disappears in white powder.
A deer's meticulous, heart-shaped footprints intersect the
trail. Gliding at modest speed I conjure: Leonardo on Swan
Mountain, prototypes of flying machines inhabit his brain. Old
tales of falling, surfacing from where they've slept, inhabit mine:
Adam and Eve. Babel's sky-high tower. Macbeth—victorious,
valiant, loyal—before he vaulted and o'er-leapt. An angel, light-
robed, face aglow, lifted its glorious wings and fell.

That evening at Gull Lake

we flew. Flew as if we had wings and knew
no limits. We were Olympians
shot from the mouth of a starting gun.
Hands joined, laughing at gravity,
we were a whip that whizzed
and cracked
when the anchoring blade dug in
and held. No one fell.
                    We slowed
at the marshy end where turtles bask
in summer in thick reeds,
                         then turned
and gaining speed raced the lake's length
back to where we'd laced our skates,
vying to be first on ice. We mapped
the whole of Gull Lake's wind-swept length,
its glassy breadth. With bold velocity
our blades bisected frozen fissures.
                              All of us,
exhilarated, screamed our heads off.
Our hearts were wild. Our multicoloured
toques and jackets in the moonlight monochrome
and ghostly. Suddenly
                    we saw them:
shadowy beneath our skates' knife edges,
racing us. Or fleeing. Nothing but ice
between their spectral fins, our speed.

We'd never seen fish glide through the dark
November water, the import of their presence
palpable yet veiled. Light of the half-full moon
shone eerily through wisps of cloud,
on silent fish, spooked skaters.
                              We were young,
our silver blades new-honed,
and through the darkening winter hours
the ice held.

IV. Stars to Steer By

Each life Converges to some Centre ... Emily Dickinson

Time

My father, a singular man, had time on his mind,
how little there was of it, how it sped hell-bent
for glory. *Man muss die Zeit auskaufen,** he said,
grinding grain for leghorns, filling the water trough,
humming a hymn. What was he thinking when he fell
so suddenly out of time? He'd intended to haul
crated eggs to the co-op. Instead, the droning feed-mill
stopped, the leghorns fidgeted as if they knew
they must be caught, crated, hauled to slaughter.
The enterprise, its hour come, shut down.
On the day of burial, a vicious prairie blizzard: snow,
like feathers in the morning, by evening needle-sharp.
You couldn't see the hen barn from the house. All space
obliterated. Time, completely spent, stood still.

(*We must redeem time.)

In translation

Und es rauschte als wollte es regnen.

I know what they mean, these words
my mother recited
when she heard the west wind
wrestling with poplars
and her garden needed rain.

The German word for 'wind' is missing
from what she remembered
but is implied. Isn't it
obviously intended?

I wanted to write a poem that catches
the rasp of wind assaulting aspen,
whipping lake waves into turbulence,
white water slapping shoreline rocks.
A poem in two languages, one voice.

But how do I translate
rauschen into English?

The wind blows where it chooses.
You hear its high-pitched wail, its rising
crescendo, cringe from its cold fury,
its burning summer breath. When it abates
you say: it is dying down. Now

there is silence so startling
the poem is held suspended
in the satin air. Now
it needs no foreign or familiar words,
couldn't care less for the pleasure
of text in accurate translation.

Two crows

I heard twa corbies making a mane (Anonymous)

A pair of crows perched like closed books on the wire fence.
They are reading me. Leaving me uneasy. All morning
they flapped up and down, distraught
parents, feeding their wide-mouthed fledglings
nested in the elm whose juicy leaves feed cankerworms.

I'm on the deck munching a tuna sandwich. I've clapped away
grackles, dull-witted rabbits from my lettuce.
Whatever grows lures gluttony. Whatever lives is ravenous.
Legions of forest tent caterpillars, fat slugs, aphids
in the hollyhocks. Across the dust-choked lane,

my neighbour, paper-thin from breast cancer,
brings her book to the window. After a winter of surgery
and chemo, volumes of radiation, light swims through her.
Only a miracle, she says, will shrink the canker in her chest,
and deep sleep silence the brash crows, blot out
the hungry shadow of their wings.

Prayer for the widow of a nature lover

Today I prayed for the young woman
whose husband after difficult illness died.
I didn't pray for *him* though I *have*
for months, not knowing should I
demand more time, plead for quick release
from stranglehold of limitations
or just leave it up to God.

I cannot bear the wife's grief.
Never again to sit in vigil at the hospital
where he struggled in his narrow bed to breathe,
to speak, to keep up hope. No more
medical opinions, desperate measures
to keep infection from a body robbed
by assault on blood cells gone berserk
of its immunity. In future

when she wakes, if there is sun,
it shines on places he once occupied.
Shadows fall on hills he need no longer climb.
In case of rain, forest paths she walked with him
will be as filled with water as her eyes. At every turn
sorrow will greet her.

> *Let it be portioned out*
> *in decreased doses*
> *taken with a small cup*
> *of courage*
> *a tincture of light.*

Stars to steer by

We buried the woman in a frozen portion of the planet
and drove home. The unwilling sun hung low
over Winnipeg. Wind scoured the streets.

She was poorly dressed for the weather. Ungloved hands
at rest for once, feet ice-cold, motionless,
a face as unrevealing as the moon's.

Over tea, grieving, we recited landscapes
where she might have been laid to rest. In waters
of the Dnieper River when the hydro dam blew up,

refugee camp in Yugoslavia, trapped in the Russian zone.
Might have lain with her exiled husband in permafrost,
the blood-flecked snow her shroud.

Trekking west with the retreating German army, lost,
children in tow, she became irresistible.
Dive bombers swooped like vultures

once
       twice
           again.

She herded her children into a culvert,
shoved her own head after them and waited
in the rusty dark for silence.   Dying

in Winnipeg (a lifetime later) she said
all she ever wanted was her children saved,
a face that could be recognized in death. She wanted,

rising over mud and gunfire,
an uncorrupted moon
and quiet stars to steer by.

Letter and reply
(In memory of Joan McGuire)

"Let me describe the island
where I'm dying. The ocean
always restless, always there.
A morning warbler I've not yet seen,
a soprano, sings from a thicket,
a melody of happiness that almost
overshadows pain. I'm new here,
(not new to suffering) tired, unable
to imagine spring, a green world
blossoming. Forests are orange,
crimson. The sun
burning through morning mist
radiates the body, spills over everything
light that is new and glorious
enough to die for."

"Here on the prairie, autumn's beauty
is subdued. Imagine plain brown,
modest yellow. The occasional hedge
a splash of red like recent blood.
Everything's dry, the land needs rain.
Today I'll clean the eaves for winter,
hike beside the river that in spring
overflows its boundaries. Could be

I'll see the sun set fire to the sky
before retiring. I'll unfold
your latest island letter, grateful
to know the Light you wait for in the east
(as I do in the west)
can suddenly break through,
appearing everywhere."

Waiting

(In memory of Tim Legere)

On the hospital bed, a body:
long, straight and still
breathing,
though the eyes don't open
and the ears can't hear.
No sound escapes the body's vocal cords
to slip across its lips.

Two women on straight-backed chairs
watch and wait.
The woman who is the mother naturally
insists on hoping. Says she sees
eyelashes flutter, the chest heave slightly
more than usual, lips quiver.
Believes she hears a sigh. Sees
a tinge of colour where there's pallor.

The other woman, a friend, observes
the monitor pulsing faintly,
fainter. Messages
from lungs, heart, brain
reduced to erratic graph lines.
She hears the monotonous drip
drip of fluid into plastic,
the incessant hum and whirr.

Neither woman knows for sure
the outcome of her waiting.
The IC unit's air-conditioned,
sterile, windowless.
Day after day sun blossoms in the east
and slides behind the west horizon
after supper. The women,
watching the still,
still-breathing body,
cannot see it.

Nightwatch

(In memory of Heidi Koop)

Wind rattles the empty trashcan,
slaps ghostly ash tree branches into motion,
motion triggers the dormant sensor lights,
a flare from which the startled dark recoils.
I am safe, navigating from garage to deck to door.

Inside, a single lamp left burning, beacon for the hour
when fear steals in, solitude is loneliness, and sleep,
death's counterfeit, perversely stays away.

I left you alone at midnight in that hospice room,
dozing or in a coma, breathing in and out.
Mouth open. Tubed. Monitored.
Three ghostly lights left glimmering.
Footsteps in the corridor.

Pray that it won't be long, you said, when you still could.
Today my entreaty for peace is not for the bloodied world:
It is for you. One last expended breath

and the solitary, dreaded navigation
is accomplished. Morning flares,
holds you in pure light
that will not (like a blustery autumn day)
give way to night.

What we want

Where have they gone? The quiet
bodies decomposing, burnt to ash,
scattered. Wherever
they are, they continue to exist
in photo albums, home videos,
in our hearts. We imagine them

arriving at some shore
no eye has ever seen
and no ear heard the haunting
language of its music. A country
no one's mapped, no one's travelled
and returned from.

We want them back. Or else
somewhere at rest and without fear
of AIDS, the West Nile virus, SARS.
We want them where they have no need
for respirators, wheelchairs, frequent MRIS,
puffers, pills for under the tongue,

no need to carry with them where they go
the weight of pain. Dull grudges. Guns.
Or guilt.
We want them where one day,
alive
and unencumbered,
we will find them.

Passing

We passed the school where children strove,
At recess, in the ring,
We passed the fields of gazing grain,
We passed the setting sun.   (Emily Dickinson)

Mid-morning. Sun not yet at zenith
and already over-bright. West breezes,
green meadows and that wide road
an open invitation. A feisty finch sang
and we believed everything possible,
time without end. Beside a poplar grove
we stopped for lunch, still wondering
was this trip pleasure? Was it pilgrimage?
Bulrushes beside us, the unwrinkled sky above,
we passed the school where children strove

at baseball. They fought like cats. Or laughed.
We watched until the buzzer called them in
to lessons. Ours, we believed, long past.
Was it geometry or history we hated? Did we
love to bring our finger-painted sunsets home?
Were we read poetry? Did we sing?
We reached an intersection. Right or left?
We had to choose and couldn't. Getting late.
Far to go and we were back and forth, arguing
like kids *at recess, in the ring.*

One way or another, we moved on. Was it right?
Was it wrong? We upped our pace.
Might have been on foot we went, by bike
or motorized. Not like Emily, horse-drawn
in her tulle tippet. We turned, uneasily,
to her poetry, none of us ready to name
the goal of that slow carriage ride. Instead:
the thing with feathers, slant of light, her white
dress delighted us. Not yet in any haste
we passed the fields of gazing grain

ready for harvest. Someone said, It's death
poets always write about, citing as evidence
the fly buzzing, the Loaded Gun, the ominous
Hour of Lead. Truth was, none of us knew
what cities, oil wells, accidents the road might
take us past. Or through. Long shadows following us,
we started singing. Not sadly, but softly, more or less
in harmony. We'd found (perhaps were given) our voices.
Above us, the first bright star, just
as *we passed the setting sun.*

Road trip

You've made good headway on the highway
when the first drops fall, followed by the deluge.
Sheets of water batter the asphalt. Wild clover,
grasses violated. Barley yellow for harvest
flattened. Water-logged. But you, you'll make it
to your destination, windshield wipers lashing
out. It's dark, your boots mud-caked by the time
you stumble to the door. But never mind: this
is your home. It's dry. Warm. Power is on,
tea steeps while the downpour turns to hail, pellets
rattle the windows, the whole cowed world opaque.
Had you pictured homecoming differently? Sun-lit,
perhaps? Someone there to welcome you, to ask you
where in the world you've been and did you really
think you'd ride through storm unharmed, unsullied,
a conqueror, alone? Well, did you? Put your feet up.
Circle the steaming mug with your cold fingers.
Forget the rain-clogged fields, the ruined harvest.
A traveller needs respite on the narrow road
to Egypt. To the new Jerusalem. Or home.

V. The Potter

Faith requires a question—

or at the very least, the absence of an answer.
                    Yi-Mei Tsiang

The shepherd's wish list

Barely midnight. All of us hunkered down
like hoboes around ashes of a fire. The animals
asleep. Our companions: hunger, nagging doubt.
Our wants are reasonable: provisions for the family,
better health, a better bed than this hard slope,
good grazing, sturdy lambs, and death to predators
whose hostile howls invade our restless dreams.
But let's be honest: let's admit right now:

what we want most is fool-proof evidence
that God exists and knows we're here. We want
our sorrows noted, our frantic labours recognized.
We want the Holy One, although it's dark (and late
the hour) to hunker with us at the fire's glow
and speak with us—Right here. Right now.

New wool and old

A prairie farmer ships one and a half
sheep's off-white shearing
to a factory in PEI. The wool is washed,
carded, spun, machine-woven into a thick blanket,
dyed red as a rooster's comb, an inflamed tongue,
open wounds in Kabul, Jerusalem,
New York. An inner-city

thrift store gets the worn sweater you knitted
that summer at the lake when sky opened
and it poured. How you rued the dismal
hours. Skein after skein the wool slipped
through your fingers. When finally the sun
broke through, you joined front to back,
sewed in the sleeves. That sleeveless,

ancient cloak—who'd gamble for it?
Stripped from the mutilated back of one
who has no further use for it. Sweaty,
stained brown with blood, handwoven
seamlessly of good wool, it is durable and still
warm. Soldiers throwing dice around the fire
know: it cannot be divided.

The potter

So I went down to the potter's house,
and I saw [her] working at the wheel. (Jeremiah 18:3)

Coming in from the wind, dishevelled, we cluster
like commas around the woman at the wheel.
Her foot moves up and down. Hands cup the clay,
centring, altering, coaxing it upward. We grow alert
as exclamation points. The matter in the potter's hand
gains shape: a bowl, lip like a wing, round belly.
Her fingers cradle the emerging form, emending it
to match the brain's vision. The alluring

object, as we watch, collapses in the brackets
of her hands. With one swift move she scoops it up,
squashes it, a mundane blob of clay.
She doesn't say: *That's it. Period.*
To question marks surrounding her, she says
she'll rescue that smashed lump tomorrow,
rises, unties the denim apron stained with a residue
of clay, rinses her hands,

                            waves us to the table.
Coffee is poured into mugs she has made.
Oatmeal raisin cookies, lemon drops. We eat
and leave a scattering of crumbs to punctuate
the lucent pearl-blue glaze of perfect plates
that only yesterday our gracious potter
pulled with her stained, shard-lacerated hands
from the fire.

Medium of choice

Eons ago a mountain range reigned,
serene, unseen except by oversized
prehistoric creatures now long gone
from landscapes north of Thompson,

Manitoba. The cold rolled in. Over-
powering glaciers sheared away
those austere peaks, altering geography.
Huge chunks of rock, loose gravel

jammed together, packed in ice,
metamorphosed. Conglomerates
of granite, basalt, shale flowed south,
to be deposited in places east of Morden,

Manitoba. The artist from Altona
hauls to his stone-free acreage—ancient
lake-bottom—boulders from glacial deposits,
transports slabs of granite from Big Whiteshell Lake.

Like Michelangelo's his medium of choice
has weight, girth, substance. And like
a potter eyeing a mundane lump of clay,
he envisions in what's drab, formless,

the nascent shape of beauty and utility.
Marshalling his power tools, imagination,
good sense, muscle, he goes to work
not knowing the outcome. He dreams

the shape of what is aching to emerge,
hopes what is imagined
and what is ultimately made
will be like clasped hands, one.

In the garden

*Then God said, "Let us make humankind
in our image..."* (Genesis 1:26)

What were you thinking, God? In spring
the boulevards strut their tenderest green
spun in your brain. Tantalizing birdsong,
fragrances float straight to the head. The heart,
as you well know, falters.
We'll regularly fail to tend the garden,
forget to feed the animals. Apples
will be wasted. How extravagantly

beautiful the blossoms are on shrubs and trees
in May. Impatient, we want fruit, not green,
but glowing. Want to sink our teeth
into the flesh of apricots. Our tongues crave
taste of apples.

What were you thinking, leaving us in charge,
giving us dominion, as if we were fit
to be emperors, chief executives, micro or macro
managers, as if we understood
words like *tend, wait patiently* and *multiply?*

As if we were able with our wayward minds
to imagine mercy's breadth and wideness,
had ears to hear, could learn to linger
long enough to taste and see.

Scenarios

1.

First possible scenario:
a word is spoken, invocation to the roiling,
bubbling darkness. Presto—light!
Life bursts into being, bright, curious,
afloat in crystal water, slugging
through mud (like molasses), a marathon
of creeping, crawling, full-out flight.
A world in half a dozen super-busy days
made out of nothing.

The second (also plausible):
divine hands cover divine ears,
while the deafening BANG
triggers an abrupt awakening
followed by snail-paced evolving,
adapting: moss on rock, bread fruit
with its diverse uses, panda, koala,
those fascinating floating creatures
we call devil's knitting needles.

Either way the intrepid buds
that open pink and white in May,
give way to fruit that ripens, glows,
tempts. In time's fullness
we bring harvest home,
rejoicing. Then grieve
the annual dying down.

Once again it's spring and in the morning,
naked as that pair in Eden,
we stare at that same blossoming
scenario, startled. Utterly
dumbfounded.

2.

Did God for whom time stretches like elastic
or shrinks like snow beneath the sun
(or makes no matter)
know: sometime, someplace
a bus would slide from a slick highway,
crush its cargo of school children, seniors
on their way to a spring picnic,
winter skiers headed for the slopes, all
vibrant or frail hope?

An aircraft falls, a flaming
meteor out of the blue
or a ship collides with the invisible
portion of a crystal ice mass
leaving the world (aghast)
counting the souls lost.

Let's say one individual escapes.
Survives. Is
pulled from wreckage, water, fire,
alive. A miracle.
Why only one and why *this* one?
We want to know: who
reaps praise for rescue? Who
gets blamed for all the rest?

3.

When everything fails:
the garden made with hope and good seed
won't sprout, shrivels, gets rained out,
the body's functions falter, the economy collapses,
the engine dies and you miss the opening
of Haydn's *Creation*, a baseball game,
the last flight out,
when in spite of peace marches and prayer vigils
the nations rage furiously, barraging
hospitals, fields where children play
with death, and love
is helpless, in scant supply,
flatly refused,

oh then you want the sky opened,
divinity revealed.
You want the Almighty's muscle
flexed,
a strong arm reaching out,
reaching down to you. Instead,
resounding silence. You are left with
nagging questions, tattered faith
that flickers now and then,
sputters, falters
and (sometimes) like a nearly-dying fire
is by a stir of wind
revived
and like that fabled desert bush
flames out.

St. Peter's Abbey: *Ora et labora*

The bells again: calling all brothers
to the chapel. Devout feet measure
patiently familiar distances
between hard labour, honest prayer.
Oversized leather boots, work-worn
track shoes, ridiculous white
socks in loafers, inches of frayed jeans
below sombre skirts.

They were busy in canola fields
and in the garden tending onions,
radishes, red runner beans.
Summoned by the abbey bells they
clambered down from trucks, tractors,
unbent their bodies from the earth. Stopped
wrestling with weeds, cutworms, God.
Washed their hands, clothed themselves
in quietness. In robes the colour of earth.

When the bells stop tolling, tenor,
bass and baritone chant litanies of praise,
intone confession and petition. The monks
bring with them to the chapel their desire,
their celibate devotion. Also despair.
When they rise from their knees, modest
residues of earth fall from their feet,
seeds scatter, that should have been covered with soil
and left to die. To rise again, green.

Their shod feet carry them—resigned
or joyful—back to work,
leaving the empty sanctuary
redolent: scent of new-mown hay,
the sour smell of sweat rise
like incense drifting heavenward
or falling back to earth.

St. Peter's Abbey: *Deo volente*

The farmer-monk wants clean crops
of corn, canola. He wants
to eradicate blight, grubs,
noxious weeds rampant
in every acre. He discovers
it can't be done.

The gardener-monk pulls
from among perennials
purple loosestrife, thistles
that multiply and choke the life
out of lupine and dianthus.

All night wheat and weeds grow
side by side, delphiniums
and dandelions thrive equally.
In summer fields quack grass
invades canola.

It's not yet Eden,
the farmer mutters. Not quite
perfection, grumbles the gardener.

Both rise early, scan the sky,
and shield their anxious eyes
against the searing sun that beats down
everywhere, equally.
They kneel for morning prayer:

Give us for God's sake one
whole night of steady rain
to soften stone-hard soil
nourish parched roots
raise blades of hope
and guarantee the harvest.

The race

To the one who conquers... (Book of Revelation)

You are at the beach, reading. Increasing winds
riffle the lake's grey page, puff out slack sails
at the regatta starting line. The windsurfer's wet
suit gleams and the plastic sail he grasps crackles.
Clouds take the shape of an Olympic swimmer
seen in the pool from below, executing the crawl,
arms reaching out like overeager wings. A whistle
signals the start of the race. Let's say the open

book is a Bible. A breeze flips the pages,
Genesis to Revelation, a narrative that holds
within it both the sailor and the sail. Are you
surprised it ends in metaphor? Not a cup
but a crown. Your new name plainly carved
in white stone. The promised morning star.

At the window, reading

I am at the window, reading. The material
substance of this hard-cover copy, scuffed
flooring underneath my feet, my shoulder
comforted by sun, peaches in a silver bowl,
can be broken down with known technology
or theory to subatomic particles, the subject of
this book reduced to bits of information, subtexts,
the air I breathe to gaseous components
no one can see or smell.

My neighbour smiles when she arrives,
buttered muffins on a plastic plate,
toddler barnacled to her leg. Such gestures
too are deconstructible. Evolutionary
psychologists declare: goodness, scrutinized,
is shown to spring forth weed-like from self-serving
hunger for reward or the animal impulse *to perpetuate
genetic material.*

There goes that old couple,
he with a white cane, she stricken with Alzheimer's,
walking their leashed Doberman down the lane
like every blessed morning. Shall I wave from the window?
Run out to say hello?

What's at the root of everything? Long-delayed
plans to refinish the scuffed pine floor, finish the book
I'm reading (*Rumours of Another World*),
catch the sun's warm rays. What is it impels me
to claim without delay
the juicy promise of this peach?

Within

You yourself are even another little world
and have within you the sun and the moon
and even the stars. (Origen)

Within me is the desert,
its vast, dry distances. Within me,
the uneven teeth of a mountain range
and also the emerald valley
where cattle graze.

Within me: silence
and a shrill chorus
demanding war.
Demanding territory.

Within: a radiant universe
and that dark continent
where everything imagination
in its brightest moments made
is blotted out.

I am a sphere of light
and deep inside me dwells
a turbulent diversity
of clouds.

I am a multitude.
And lonely.

Credo

I wanted the soprano
when she sang Handel's aria
not to be alarmed by the intruding
street noises, heat, the unrelenting
worms that one day will destroy
her body and mine.
I wanted her to disregard latecomers
trust the technique she had so far
and so well mastered.
I wanted her to believe the incredible
phrases she sang flawlessly:
> *I know that my redeemer liveth*
> *And in my flesh*
> *Shall I see God.*

In the stifling sanctuary's
last, shadowed row
I wanted
(as the thirsty deer want water)
to believe it too.

Waging peace

How beautiful on the mountains are the feet
of the messenger who announces peace. (Isaiah 52:7)

Not something separate. Not
a convenient screen, walls hastily thrown up
to keep a conflict's blaze contained.
Or the self safe.

Not something hammered out at tables.
And never sentimental, say a moonlit evening,
incandescent sky or the wide Pacific Ocean
on a breathless night. You might as well

wage peace as war. You'll have to stand
exposed at the crossroads of unguarded anger
a presence, not an absence.
Not gritting your teeth,

not forcing your clenched hands
open. Your heart's timid core
and everything the stubborn mind conceals,
revealed. Disarmed

you become disarming,
the terror in your unmasked face
radiant. Your unshod, wounded feet
beautiful.

Night sky at Deep Bay

Midnight, and the sky above the lake
ablaze with a zillion fires lit while I slept.
Each flame a declaration, each solemn planet bright.
I tilt my head way back, and there's The Milky Way,
there's Cassiopeia, Orion, Ursa Major, the Pleiades,
a whole bright host.

Years ago while snow fell quietly on Latvia,
I entered the majestic Riga Dom.
From the balcony a choir sang, a capella,
from Schubert's *Deutsche Messe*,
the *Sanctus*.

The Baltic Sea slept
while the sanctuary's hushed, cold corners
overflowed with: Holy, Holy, Holy
and our eyes with tears.

On the beach tonight I shiver, not with cold,
but overcome—unwitting witness
to the firmament's explosion—with astonishment.
As if the host of Bethlehem's angels
and the celestial Latvian voices joined
to wake the midnight world
with radiant, resounding Glorias.

(When I am old or ill
will all the stars be there, still
burning, still untarnished,
declaring truth and beauty
are not dead, not even dormant?
And will that choir sing?)

Fireworks on New Year's Eve

This diamond cold invokes our childhood
skating days: numb feet, metallic scrape of blades
on ice, shrill screams when the strung-out skaters hurtled past
and the whip cracked. Against tonight's black sky

the first flamboyant vision flares: we gasp,
crane our muffled necks, eyeing, oohing
the fantasy. The brittle darkness dissipates,
replaced by a burst of spiralling begonias,

resplendent roses, gold dahlias, birds
of a winter paradise. The blossoming
gives way to incandescence: red, white, blue
extravaganzas to inflame the ardent heart.

Beneath our feet the snow,
a crumpled, grungy bed sheet.
The narrow street a crunch of tires,
ice-tunnel of exhaust.

And we, no longer children, shiver,
done with the fiery sky, done with the bone-deep
cold. We want a warm car, warm room,
a table set for all of us.

We want a new year, yes, but want it
without fanfare. Let it come
into our slendered lives with muted music,
mellow candle light.

Before our clocks flip over
at the stroke of midnight, bring us wine
and let us sip contentment. Before we sleep
give us to taste the bread of peace.

Acknowledgements

I wish to thank Jamis Paulson and Sharon Caseburg for their encouragement and kind attention to my manuscript. Deep thanks also to Alice Major, who read the manuscript with such care and edited with rigour and wisdom.

Some of these poems have appeared in the following magazines: *CV2*, *Event*, *Direction*, *Geez*, *Image*, *MB Herald*, *Prairie Fire*, and in the following anthologies: *Pith & Wry* (ed. Susan McMaster, Scrivener Press, 2010); *Northern Lights* (ed. Byron Rempel-Burkholder and Dora Dueck, Wiley, 2008); *Poetry as Liturgy* (ed. Margo Swiss, St. Thomas, 2007); *a/cross sections* (ed. Katherine Bitney and Andris Taskans, Manitoba Writers' Guild, 2007); *Imagine a World: Poetry for Peacemakers* (compiled by Peggy Rosenthal, Pax Christi USA, 2005); *Waging Peace* (ed. Susan McMaster, Penumbra, 2002).

Notes

"Monstrance," "*Purim*" and "Guide to the KGB museum" were shortlisted for the CBC Literary Award. Between the two world wars, Vilnius was considered the Jewish capital of eastern Europe. *Purim* is a Jewish holiday that celebrates the victory recounted in the book of Esther in the Hebrew scriptures. The line "eternity in pulsing hearts" is a reference to Ecclesiastes 3:11 NIV. "Birthday party" alludes to the execution of Saddam Hussein on December 30, 2006. "Stars to steer by" alludes to *Going by the Moon and the Stars: Stories of two Russian Mennonite Women* by Pamela E. Klassen, Wilfrid Laurier University Press, 1994, and is dedicated to all the women who took part in the Great Trek out of the Soviet Union to the west in the 1940s. The artist in "The potter" is Barbara Wiebe. The artist in "Medium of choice" is Todd Brown. "At the window, reading" alludes to *Rumours of Another World* by Philip Yancey. "Falcon" was partly inspired by *Married to a Bedouin*, a memoir by Marguerite van Geldermalsen.

"Blankets for Afghanistan" is for Martha Klassen; "Home invasion" is for Gwen Macdonald; "Molly Magoo" is for Norma McCurdy; "Songs of Ascent" is for Evelyn Labun; "That evening at Gull Lake" is for the Bakers; "Prayer for the widow of a nature lover" is for Linda Dyck; "New wool and old" is for Bonnie Loewen; "Night sky at Deep Bay" is for Esther Wiens; "Fireworks on New Year's Eve" is for Agnes Dyck, Anne DeFehr, Kate Kehler and Winnie Warkentin.